The Magic of Borneo

CONTENTS

The Island of Borneo

With all its cultural and natural diversity, Borneo is a place few visitors leave without taking a little piece of it away in their hearts. Its singular creatures, from sandy-haired, angel-eyed orang-utans to clumsy (harmless) leeches, and its natural habitats, from glorious rainforests to mountains and rivers, constitute a natural heritage that becomes increasingly precious and ever more worthy of experiencing at first hand. Cultural diversity is not only striking in its own right but remarkably accessible, especially in Sarawak and Sabah where English has become a common means of communication, and visitors from every part of the world are welcomed.

Above It is estimated that there are around 3000 species of wild orchid surviving on the island of Borneo, about ten per cent of the world's total. Their habitat ranges from the lowland swamp forests to the huge dipterocarp forests, and they are particularly diverse in the forests which line the majestic rivers on the island.

Left Trees in the rainforest are home to thousands of plant and animal species. Orchids find homes in the branches while forest creepers use their trunks as a climbing frame. The tree on the left has been cleared of its climbers and epiphytes while that on the right is in its natural state.

Right A Kayan hunter uses a blowpipe to catch the family's lunch. The Kayan tribe live in longhouses on the borders of Sarawak and Kalimantan and make up one per cent of Sarawak's total population. They make a living as rice farmers.

Left Life along the rivers of Kalimantan has changed little over the years. Families live alongside the river which forms their highway into town, their source of drinking water, and provides much of their food.

Below A beach jetty at Pulau Sapi, one of the five islands that make up Tunku Abdul Rahman Park – a nature reserve off the coast of Kota Kinabalu on Sabah. It is a popular holiday resort with the local people.

Occupying a large archipelago that lies between the Indian and Pacific oceans, Borneo is the third largest island in the world. Its three-quarters of a million square kilometres consist of a number of different states of which the smallest is the independent and oil-rich sultanate of Brunei. Next in size come the two states of Sabah and Sarawak, known as East Malaysia but separated from mainland Peninsular Malaysia by hundreds of miles of sea. By far the largest part of Borneo, about three-fourths of the island, is Kalimantan, which forms a part of Indonesia.

Borneo may nowadays be merely a geographical, rather than a political term, but the sound of its name retains a hold on the imagination that transcends its national territories. It conjures up strange and almost mystical images of wild 'dreamforests' filled with fabulous creatures, fierce head hunters and glistening rivers that flow between misty mountains.

Even though, today, Borneo is able to offer the modern tourist every conceivable creature comfort, it can still claim an Eden-like association – an enchanting land where nature has expressed herself in her most extravagant, fragrant and colourful form.

GEOGRAPHY

Millions of years ago, during the Pleistocene period, Borneo formed part of Sundaland, a vast continent made up of Southeast Asia and the Indonesian archipelago. As sea levels rose at the end of the last Ice Age, Borneo and its diverse wildlife became cut off from the mainland. Mountains in the centre of the island were dissected by slow-moving wide rivers that, in turn, were surrounded by low-lying, swampy and relatively infertile soil. It is geographical features such as these that made travel slow and commercial exploitation prohibitively expensive, thus serving to protect what remains of Borneo's indigenous cultures and wildlife.

Borneo's highest mountain is Gunung Kinabalu (4101m; 13,455ft) in Sabah. Sections of this granite mound are yet to be completely explored

Right The entrance to Clearwater Cave in Gunung Mulu, Sarawak. The cave is 107km (66 miles) long, the longest in Southeast Asia. It was discovered in 1988. At its entrance is the pool of water which gives it its name.

Right Sayat Sayat hut on the slopes of Mount Kinabalu – at 3666m (12,028ft) it is the last stop before the summit; there is little or no vegetation. Many climbers make the journey in the hours before dawn so that they can see the sunrise from the mountain's peak.

and still pose a challenge to the world's most experienced mountaineers.

Mountain ranges run east to west across the island, which is mercifully outside the 'ring of fire' earthquake belt that encompasses the rest of the Indonesian islands. To the northwest and northeast of Borneo lie large deposits of oil that have helped to make Brunei one of the wealthiest states in the world.

In the northeast of Sarawak, Mulu National Park contains a mixture of sandstone and limestone mountains, riddled with caves and the strange geological formations called karst. These sharply pointed pillars are 45m (147ft) high in some cases and project through the mountain vegetation. Beneath the mountains lie vast cave systems, some as long as 50km (31 miles) and many as yet unexplored. Sarawak Chamber, part of this system, is the largest known cave cavity in the world.

CLIMATE

Since Borneo is situated in its fortunate position close to the equator, it avoids the typhoons that affect countries to the north and south. The island's climate follows typical monsoon patterns, except when El Niño enforces drought conditions. When it rains between November and January, rivers often burst their banks and become unnavigable. Even in the dry season, Borneo experiences some rain every day and receives between 1140–3050mm (45–120in) of rain per year. The monsoon winds sweep across the South China Sea from the mainland and pick up their load of water as they travel, shedding it on the island in bursts of rain which would shock those of us from more moderate climates. Sadly, in recent years, the failure of the winter monsoon has resulted in tinder-dry vegetation, and terrible forest fires have wiped out entire swathes of virgin forest. The dry season, which lasts until September, is brought on by drier winds crossing the Australian continent.

The heavy rainfall has partly accounted for Borneo's geography, eroding the mountains and creating river-cut valleys. Temperatures average between 25–30°C (77–86°F), day and night, throughout the year. Humidity is high, even in the mountains, where temperatures can drop to 6°C (43°F).

Below The beautiful, hibiscus flowers provide nectar for many of the island's creatures.

Right Danum Valley, 43km² (17 sq miles) of rainforest in southern Sabah, is home to 200 species of trees per hectare, 275 species of birds, and 110 species of mammals.

COASTLINE, REEFS AND BEACHES

Borneo has thousands of miles of coastline, tracts of white sandy beaches backed by luscious tropical vegetation, supporting tiny fishing villages and the occasional luxurious tourist resort. Travellers can live out their dreams of beach holidays with all the paraphernalia: windsurfing, paragliding and getting bronzed while sipping tall iced drinks.

Many of the beaches are set in national parks where wildlife is protected and strange species such as pitcher plants, rhinoceros hornbills, proboscis monkeys and hawksbill turtles live – unaware of the human activity that surrounds them.

In sheltered river estuaries are mangrove swamps where mangrove trees perch with their roots in salt water, supporting a delicate ecosystem of creatures such as mudskippers – curious amphibious fish that flit about on the mud at low tide, as happy out of water as they are in it. The mangroves, too, are strange life forms, absorbing salt through their roots and excreting it from their twigs and leaves.

Offshore are acres of coral reefs, supporting yet more fragile and unworldly creatures. The most accessible for travellers are the coral gardens of Tunku Abdul Rahman Park, five islands just off the coast of Kota Kinabalu in Sabah. Requiring a little more effort to explore are the reefs that surround Pulau Sipadan which supports a vast variety of reef fish, leopard- and hammerhead sharks, as well as sea turtles.

Below Kota Kinabalu (KK) harbour is the setting-off point for trips to Tunku Abdul Rahman Park, Brunei and Pulau Labuan, a tiny duty-free island off the coast of KK popular with divers for its off-shore WW II wrecks.

Above Around the many coral reefs which survive along the coasts and offshore islands of Borneo, shoals of beautifully coloured fish are common.

Above Some of the many species of palms inhabiting the Bako National Park in Sarawak rely on the rapid decomposition of forest debris for nutrients.

Below *Nepenthes edwardsiana* has a hollow cup containing a liquid which drowns any unsuspecting insect that falls in, and digests it.

FLORA

The steamy tropical climate of Borneo has encouraged a vast and unique collection of flora and fauna. Thousands of plants and animals are found only on this island and have no other environment outside of Borneo. Many of them have never been identified or conclusively studied.

Sadly, the alarming rate at which many of these rare species are being extinguished is well documented. Around 100 years ago, 95 per cent of the island was covered in healthy primary rainforest. A century of mining, logging and raging fires have reduced the virgin forest areas significantly, robbing many plants and animals of their natural habitat.

State governments are well aware of this danger. As a result, a significant number of national parks and reserves have been specially created in an effort to redress the balance and preserve Borneo's unique natural splendour.

Above Blossoms of the Aeschyanthus is one of the many beautiful plants that can be seen at Batu Apoi Forest Reserve in Brunei.

WILDLIFE

Once common in jungles from southern China to Java, orang-utans are now found only in the lowland forests of Borneo and Sumatra. Due to their accessibility, these forests provide little protection and, as a result, orang-utan populations are threatened. Their exact numbers are not known, but with infant animals fetching up to US$60,000 on the black market, the future of the entire species is under grave threat.

Orang-utans are solitary creatures, living and nesting in the canopy of the forest. These gentle, intelligent vegetarians are remarkably human-like in appearance and behaviour (*orang-utan* is Malay for 'man of the forest'). They have a life span of about 30 years and females produce an infant roughly every seven years. Visitors to Sarawak and Sabah can see orang-utans in one of the rehabilitation centres where young orphans and those that have been rescued from captivity are reintroduced to the wild. Many of them are so accustomed to human company that they have to be taught to be wary of the visitors.

I cherish the memory of my first trip to the rehabilitation centre at Sepilok in Sabah, where a young male orang-utan shuffled onto the pathway beside me, took my hand with a firm grip – an adult male has the strength of seven human males – and accompanied me through the jungle.

Orang-utans that live around the headquarters of the sanctuaries can be mischievous. Snatching cameras, hats or sunglasses from unwary visitors, they dance off into the canopy, waving their prize at the baffled visitors below.

Another famous Bornean creature, the proboscis monkey, also lives in the lowland forests as well as in mangrove swamps. These creatures are shy and difficult to observe;

Right Black-and-orange trilobite beetles feed on the decaying wood of the forest floor. They are also found on the slopes of Mount Kinabalu.

Left Baby orang-utans at Sepilok Orang-utan Sanctuary are protected from those people who still hunt them for sale as pets.

visitors are most likely to spot them on a river trip, where they can be seen foraging for leaves and shoots in the trees, making a distinctive honking noise like geese. They live in troops or harems dominated by one male, and a gang of youngsters who will eventually leave the pack and find their own females. The distinctive feature of the male proboscis monkey is its enormous red nose. Strangely, for a creature that eats only leaves, proboscis monkeys can, and do, swim – they even have webbed feet.

Since visitor numbers at Danum Valley Conservation Area in Sabah are restricted, trips to the relatively new Kinabatangan Wildlife Sanctuary are a welcome alternative. Here, tourists may spot a wide variety of Bornean wildlife, including elephants. Theories abound as to how these pachyderms came to be native on an island, so far from the rest of their kind. One theory suggests that elephants have lived on Borneo for millions of years (at one time land bridges connected the island to mainland Asia), another suggests that they are descended from tame elephants given to the Sultan of Sulu by the East India Company.

Other animals present in the sanctuary include orang-utan, gibbons, monkeys, crocodiles and some 200 species of birds.

Visitors to rural Borneo may hear and see one of its most unusual birds, the hornbill. Of Borneo's eight different types, the rhinoceros hornbill is one of the noisiest and most spectacular. With a large upturned casque atop its beak, it flies over the forest with whooshing wing beats, honking rather loudly. Rhinoceros hornbills are famous for being monogamous, and for the fact the breeding females seclude themselves in mud-walled nests, leaving only a tiny slit through which males offer food. They hatch a single egg in the dark confines of a tree trunk.

Below The disproportionately sized bill of this hornbill is surmounted by a hollow 'casque' which has no practical purpose; it is thought to be used for recognition of species.

Above The proboscis monkey, *Nasalis larvatus*, is confined to the lowland swamp and riverine forests of Borneo. The male can be spotted amongst the trees because of its distinctive white tail. Proboscis monkeys live in harems – one male with up to 40 females.

The Human Rainbow

The approximately 12 million people who live on the island of Borneo make up a glorious ethnic rainbow. Most live along a narrow strip of land around the coast and along major river courses that serve as the island's highways.

THE DAYAKS

The interior of the island, mostly dark forested mountains, is largely inhabited by the Dayaks, an Indonesian term for Kalimantan's indigenous population – 200 or more tribes of pale-skinned, small-boned people, who traditionally practise a shifting agriculture in the form of hunting and slash-and-burn farming. Some, like the remaining Penans of Sarawak, are purely hunter-gatherers, owning only what they can carry and migrating from one part of the forest to another. The more settled Dayaks live in traditional wooden longhouses, although many now work for logging or mining companies, own four-wheel-drive vehicles and dress in jeans and T-shirts rather than cloth woven from forest materials. Dayak people once practised a form of animism and many of the artefacts that visitors can now buy are copies of once sacred objects. Although most Dayaks have given up the old beliefs and turned to Christianity or Islam, some – especially in Kalimantan – still profess an animist faith called *Kaharingan*, which is recognized as an official religion by the government of Indonesia.

Above A chief of one of the Dayak tribes of Kalimantan wears the traditional headdress of his rank.

Left A Dayak woman from Kalimantan wears a beaded dress and headdress, retaining the tribe's traditional fashions and motifs. Dayaks are largely animist or Christian by religion.

MALAYS AND CHINESE

The inhabitants of the towns that pepper Borneo's coastline are largely ethnic Chinese or Malay, with Sabah also home to Kadazan Dusuns and many Filipino emigrants. The Malays, who migrated to the island over hundreds of years from what is now Peninsular Malaysia, are Muslim and live settled existences. They tend to work in the timber industry and on plantations. The Chinese arrived mainly as traders and tend to be the economically dominant group. In Indonesia, ethnic tensions are rife between Chinese and non-Chinese citizens, unlike Sarawak and Sabah where peaceful multiculturalism is a way of life.

LANGUAGE

The island has two official languages which are closely related, Bahasa Malaysia and Bahasa Indonesia, but Chinese dialects are also spoken and hundreds of indigenous dialects survive to this day. English is widely spoken in Sabah and Sarawak.

RELIGION

Although many of the indigenous tribes of Borneo have converted to Islam and Christianity, ancient tribal festivals are still celebrated, especially around harvest time. Among the Kadazan of Sabah, the harvest celebration is known as the Magavau ritual. It takes place in May and is conducted in an ancient Kadazan language known only to priestesses of the ancient religion. Visitors who are lucky enough to experience the festival can witness buffalo racing, perhaps wrestling as well, and will certainly be invited to enjoy the local rice wine called *tapai*.

Above The forecourt of a Chinese temple in Kuching. Chinese people on the island practise Taoism, Buddhism and in many cases, Christianity.

Right These Malay schoolgirls are from Kuching in Sarawak – 20 per cent of the population of Borneo is of Malay descent.

Culture

The magic of Borneo is inseparable from the dizzying mix of cultures inhabiting the island. Local markets display an eclectic mixture of Western goods such as toiletries and designer jeans, alongside a bewildering array of forest delicacies in the form of edible ferns and fungi, wild-boar meat, and craft products like woven baskets and wooden carvings. Cultural diversity expresses itself in a variety of ways, from stalls and shops selling traditional Chinese remedies as well as Western pharmaceuticals, to domestic architecture. In any one town, some people will live in modern apartments and brick houses, while others prefer wooden houses built on stilts over the river, traditional longhouses, or Malay bungalows.

Iban culture, which dominates Sarawak's and West Kalimantan's inland areas along the Rejang and Baram rivers, still largely centres on the longhouse community. Traditionally, Iban women stretched their ear lobes with huge gold discs, a custom that is still in evidence among older women. Their society is relatively classless and very outgoing – as any visitor to an Iban longhouse discovers at festival time such as the Gawai harvest festival. The women still hold weaving to be an important skill – weaving the ceremonial *pua kumbu*, a tie-dyed piece of cloth used as decoration in the home, and remains an essential requirement for an Iban bride. Other cultural groups create beautiful carvings such as the massive burial poles created by the Kayan and Kenyah people of Sarawak. An art form still practised by many Dayak tribes is tattooing. The markings can indicate social status as in the *aso* design of Sarawak's Kayan people – this dragon motif is reserved for those of high social status. Among women, tattoos are a more cosmetic feature: a lady of high social status would have her hands, arms and legs covered in elaborate monochrome designs (a mixture, of sugar water and soot, is punched into the skin with a bone needle). Another important aspect of Bornean culture is the *tamu*, or market, where tribal headmen 'network', and people socialize and trade at the same time. One of the most important of these markets is held at Kota Belud in Sabah.

Above An Iban tribesman is tattooed in the traditional manner. Iban make up almost one-third of Sarawak's population. Many have become Christian and live modern lives working for logging companies and in the towns.

Below A collection of *pua kumbu*, Iban traditional cloths patterned with figures from Iban mythology and used during religious ceremonies.

History

The people of Borneo were very early traders, exchanging forest produce with passing Indian merchants as early as the fourth century AD. The Indians brought Hinduism to the island; Malay traders later introduced Islam. The Chinese began stopping off in Borneo en route to India and Java some time in the seventh century, and soon Chinese settlements sprang up in the south of the island. By the 14th century, the sultanate of Brunei dominated the north of the island, while the sultanates of Kutai and Banjarmasin ruled in the south.

ARRIVAL OF THE EUROPEANS

In the 15th century, Borneo came to the attention of the European colonial powers due to its valuable produce and strategic position on the trade routes, and British and Dutch forces fought for control of the territory. For a time the British had a foothold at Banjarmasin, but were evicted by the local sultan in 1701.

By the 19th century, Borneo had become a hiding place for the many pirates targeting British and Dutch traders in the area. Both countries sought control of the island in order to hunt the pirates down, and to exploit the lucrative local trade possibilities. The Dutch concluded treaties for outposts in the south, while the flamboyant adventurer James Brooke established a British presence in the north. Coal and oil were soon discovered. Rubber, coffee and pepper became increasingly profitable industries, and a joint British-Dutch venture in the archipelago produced the Shell Trading Company.

During World War II the island of Borneo was overrun by the Japanese. Later, the island was divided into the British colony of Sarawak, the British protectorates of Sabah and Brunei, and the Indonesian state of Kalimantan. In 1963 Sabah and Sarawak became part of the Malay Federation, later Malaysia. Brunei opted to remain a British protectorate, which it did until 1984.

Above Fruit and items of basketware are laid out on display at this marketplace.

Below In front of these traditional longhouses the local people have laid out their harvest of pepper to dry in the sun.

Into the future

The period between World War II and 1965 saw a Chinese-inspired communist insurgency centred in north Kalimantan. For East Malaysia – Sabah and Sarawak – the transition from British control to becoming part of Malaysia was also fraught with ethnic unrest as various groups fought for control of the regional governments.

Further complicating factors were the claims of sovereignty from Indonesia and the Philippines, two countries with legitimate ties, both historical and ethnic, with what were to become Malaysian states.

Many people in Sabah and Sarawak resented the transition from British to Malaysian control, preferring instead to choose independence as Brunei had done. As the national government began to exploit East Malaysia's natural resources and channel profits into the economy of Peninsular Malaysia, Brunei's choice of independence became increasingly attractive and Sabah, in particular, came close to opting for independence.

Nowadays, relative harmony prevails, with oil-rich Brunei ruled by a family sultanate and both Sabah and Sarawak flourishing on the basis of their wealth of natural resources.

Kalimantan, however, has emerged in a more unfortunate position, suffering from the anti-Chinese ethnic unrest that has surfaced all over Indonesia in recent years.

Above The gates of the sultan's palace in Bandar Seri Begawan. The palace contains 1780 rooms, requires 51,490 light bulbs to light it, covers an area of 20ha (49 acres) – and is decorated with 5.6ha (14 acres) of marble. The roof is covered in 22-carat gold leaf.

Below The imposing façade of a colonial-style house graces this street in Brunei.

Following pages Sandakan, a small bustling town on the east coast of Sabah, looks out across the Sulu Sea to the Philippines.

Sabah

Sabah, next door to Sarawak, is Malaysia's second enclave on Borneo and lies slightly north of the Equator. Its capital, Kota Kinabalu, is a good stepping-off point for one of the island's most enjoyable activities – a walk up the slopes of Mount Kinabalu. A second excursion from Kota Kinabalu is a brief sea journey to the Tunku Abdul Rahman Park. Other highlights of a trip to Sabah include the Rafflesia Forest Reserve, Sepilok Orang-utan Sanctuary and the Kinabatangan Wildlife Sanctuary. From Sandakan, you can arrange a trip to the Turtle Islands Park or Lankayan Island.

Above Kota Kinabalu is a busy, modern town but is still home to some traditional ways of life. This *kampong* built of wooden huts on stilts is perched over the sea.

Left This young woman and child are from Tuaran, a small town 33km (21 miles) north of the capital of Sabah.

Right A Bajau woman wearing the traditional dress of her tribe. The costume is worn for the traditional Bajau dance called *limbai*, performed at weddings. Bajau were once seafaring people who migrated to Borneo from the Philippines.

Above The carnivorous *Nepenthes villosa* is a bizarre but beautifully coloured pitcher plant. Its pitcher-shaped leaves attract, trap and digest insects.

Above An adult macaque grooms a younger monkey's head in the Sepilok Orang-utan Rehabilitation Centre in Sabah.

Above Looking like grand, naturally occurring pillars, these mangrove trees have developed extraordinary adaptations in order to survive in the swamps.

Left Rafflesia, the largest flower in the world, can measure up to 1m (3ft) across and weigh as much as 2kg (4lb). It is parasitic and draws its nutrients from a forest vine.

Above Orang-utans usually produce one baby, but occasionally twins are born.

Above Reaching a spectacular height of 4101m (13,455ft), Mount Kinabalu is the centrepiece of Kinabalu Park. Its granite summit is worn into fantastic pinnacles and chasms through the effects of weathering, heating and cooling.

Above White-water rafting on the Padas River is definitely for the more serious adventurer who enjoys the thrill and excitement of riding the roaring rapids of the wildest river in Sabah.

Above Many religious and social customs revolve around the sea, and each year the Bajau people invite everyone to enjoy the Regatta Lepa Lepa, where they showcase their colourful traditional sailboats.

Above Tanjung Aru Beach Hotel caters for the discerning tourist who enjoys a bit of everything – good restaurants, shopping, and game arcades for children – while still being able to take in the beauty of the surrounding South China Sea.

Right Buli Sim Sim is where the town of Sandakan originated in 1879. This large village perched on stilts over the sea is chararcterized by neat wooden houses, their verandas decorated with pot plants, while little wooden boats bob on the water below.

Above The tranquil atmosphere of the State Mosque at Kota Kinabalu in Sabah. Built in 1975 and featuring the clear lines of modern Islamic architecture, it is Malaysia's second largest mosque and can accommodate 5000 worshippers.

Right Bajau children in their *kampong,* or village, in Semporna which was built on a 35,000-year-old coral reef that was lifted up and exposed through the movements in the earth's crust.

Below The lavishly decorated Puu Jih Shih Buddhist temple, is a blaze of red and gold, writhing dragons, buddhas and hundreds of lamps. Built in 1987, it is set on the hilltop above Tanah Merah, south of Sandakan town centre.

24

Above A sea turtle rests among the coral before making its arduous journey up onto the beach to lay its eggs. Turtles are a protected species in Borneo.

Right Coral growth varies according to the movement of the sea. Where the currents are strong, growth is slow, but in deeper, calm waters the coral branch in a myriad of delicate shapes.

Below At Pulau Selingan turtle eggs are collected on the beaches each day and are brought to hatcheries such as this one, where they will hatch out protected from natural predators. After the eggs have hatched the turtles are brought back to the beach where they find their way into the sea.

Following pages One of Sabah's many beautiful, pristine beaches backed with coconut palms, and in the distance the island's mountains disappear gently into the horizon.

25

Brunei

Only 120km (75 miles) from east to west, Brunei is one of the smallest countries in the world. Nearly all travellers base themselves in the capital, Bandar Seri Begawan, known simply as BSB. Here, a prime attraction is the massively expensive Omar Ali Saifuddien Mosque. The environs of BSB boast an excellent museum, some quiet beaches, and a free amusement park that adds somewhat to the Disney-like atmosphere of the country. The Peradayan Forest Reserve can be accessed by an enjoyable boat trip downriver and then by sea to the mangrove swamps.

Above Bringing home the dinner as the washing dries in the sun – a typical scene in the quiet Kampong Ayer, a stilt village on the outskirts of Bandar Seri Begawan.

Left With its minarets and dome crowned in 22-carat gold, it is no wonder the Jame' Asr Hassanil Bolkiah Mosque is the most expensive mosque in Asia.

Right His Majesty Paduka Seri Baginda Sultan Haji Hassanil Bolkiah Mu'izzaddin Waddaulah, the current ruler of Brunei, celebrates his birthday at a special ceremony held in his honour.

Above Men and young boys worship at the Omar Ali Saifuddien Mosque. They take off their shoes before entering the mosque.

Left Islam is the official religion of Brunei. The mosque therefore plays a central role in the daily life of every Muslim. Each evening the call to prayer echoes out over the ancient *kampongs* and the busy city spread out around it.

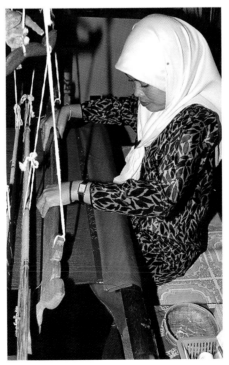

Above A bird's-eye view of the Jame' Asr Hassanil Bolkiah Mosque. Its four minarets and golden domes dominate the skyline.

Far left Kampong Ayer is the oldest part of the city and has existed in much the same form for centuries. Here fishermen sell their catch to passersby.

Left Traditional crafts on the island are as important today as they were hundreds of years ago – women still work traditional looms, weaving delicate traceries into the cloth.

Above These young men, who form the royal guard of honour, are taking part in Brunei's National Day celebrations.

Above left The National Day celebration – known as Hari Kebangsan Negara Brunei – is an important event on the calendar. This rally at the national stadium is followed by a procession, and later in the evening, a fireworks display.

Left Women soldiers participate in the national celebration, which takes place on 23 February. It is also a school holiday.

Far left Young children play an important role in celebratory processions.

Above Brunei's wealth is derived from its massive offshore oil deposits, which are vital to the continuing prosperity of its economy.

Below The Billionth Barrel Monument at Seria, Brunei's second largest town and a centre for the offshore oil industry. The monument was erected to commemorate the day when, as the name suggests, the billionth barrel of oil was drawn from the Brunei oilfields.

Above A typical street scene in BSB; its wide streets and modern housing blocks display the comfort and wealth that oil has brought to the people of this country.

Right Muslim women in traditional dress may be considered confined in their fashion taste by those in the West – but their sense of colour and design is evident in these gaily decorated dresses.

Following pages Omar Ali Saifuddien Mosque, named after the 28th Sultan of Brunei, sits on a man-made lagoon and is beautifully illuminated at night. In the foreground is a stone boat designed in the traditional fashion and used for state ceremonies.

Sarawak

Kuching, the capital of Sarawak and one of the most delightful cities in Southeast Asia, has retained its 19th-century identity in parts. Many of the public buildings are still intact and rows upon rows of Chinese shops have preserved their classical architectural form. Modern buildings have been erected in another part of the city, so you can enjoy the best of both worlds. The white rajah's palace is open to the public once a year. The interior of Sarawak is rather isolated but you can see Gunung Mulu National Park, a huge protected area, and the Kelabit Highlands – the highest inhabited region in Borneo.

Above One of the most beautiful and pleasant cities in Southeast Asia, Kuching has a thriving multicultural population. These teenagers have much the same interests as teenagers everywhere.

Left A plaque to White Rajah, Charles Brooke, who ruled the protectorate from 1842 to his death in 1917.

Right The Sarawak River dominates life in Kuching. Away from the modern city and business district, this quiet *kampong*-style community has lived along its shores for generations.

Above Fresh fish is delivered each day to the wetmarket. Here you can haggle over the prices, gossip with your neighbours and hear all the local news.

Above Freshly ground spices are displayed here, each labelled with its local name. Shoppers can have their spices mixed into their own curry flavours.

Above Tourists stop on their journey to admire the amazing karst limestone pinnacles on the slopes of Gunung Api in Mulu National Park. In places the pinnacles reach a height of 45m (148ft) and look like a forest carved out of stone.

Left The people of Kuching are among the friendliest and most tolerant people in the world, and a visit to the capital is an experience not to be missed.

Above The modern development along the Sungei Sarawak riverbank reveals paved walkways, cafés and foodstalls where locals walk in the cool of the evening, catch the ferry across to the north bank or take their evening meal in the shade of one of the pavilions.

Above The Tua Pek Kong Temple, built in 1876, is the oldest of its kind in Kuching and is famous for its Wang Kang celebrations which honour the spirits of the dead.

Right The modern Masjid Negeri, or State Mosque, dominates the city. Islam, Christianity, Hinduism and Taoism exist happily side by side in this tolerant state.

Above These Iban men will gladly don the traditional headgear of their tribe for festive occasions. Tattooing is as popular in modern times as it has been in the past.

Right Among the Iban it was believed that the heads of enemies captured in battle brought strength and protection to the longhouse. Skulls hanging at the front door are reminders of the ancient ways of these people.

Above A longhouse community on the Engkari River. Roofs that once would have been made of *attap* are now built out of more modern and durable materials, but the style of construction is much the same as it has always been.

Left Visitors to the Mulu National Park in Sarawak can travel by canoe along the Melinau River to see the amazing formations of stalactites and stalagmites in the caves.

Above The Iban people have retained their many craft skills and adapted them to modern times. These intricate bead necklaces, which would once have been made of tiny pieces of precious stone and bone, are now made of plastic beads – but are still as beautiful.

Above Women displaying the many ethnic styles of dress of Sarawak take part in a dance performance in the capital city.

Following pages The old ways of Sarawak have been protected in places such as Biduyah Cultural Village. These girls are wearing one of the many tribal dresses of the area.

Coastal Sarawak

From Kuching, an excursion northward to the coast of Sarawak brings the visitor to Bako National Park, an area of outstanding beauty that takes in deserted beaches with ancient, weathered rock formations, high hill walks with stunted trees and an abundance of carnivorous pitcher plants, proboscis monkeys, hornbills and gangs of macaques. Slightly to the west of Bako is the Santubong peninsula, another area of beaches and breathtaking beauty which has been developed into a tourist resort and nature reserve.

Above Around the beaches of Sarawak many tourist resorts have sprung up, allowing visitors to enjoy the beauty of the countryside during the day, then retire to their pretty, air-conditioned beach chalets in the evening.

Left An amusing diversion on a beach trip are the loud and quite silly hornbills which fly at a snail's pace across the beaches. Perched within the trees at the beach's edge each evening, these birds make their sonorous and raucous calls to one another.

Right Damai Beach is a very popular place with the local people at weekends. Here you can see the various ethnic groups enjoying the beach in their own way – the Malay girls as covered up in the sea as out of it, happily tolerating the shorts and T-shirts of their Chinese neighbours.

Left A view of the Cultural Village at Damai. Building styles, arts and crafts, and cultures of the various tribes of Sarawak are represented in one location.

Far left The Penan, once one of the world's few remaining nomadic groups have, controversially, been settled by the government in longhouses. Today they sell rattan baskets to tourists visiting Mulu National Park.

Below The enormous, buttressed root of a tree in the jungle of Bako National Park.

Right Visitors to Bako National Park may regret meeting these lively long-tailed macaques – which have become very tame, but have great fun stealing food from the picnic tables.

Far right One of the more challenging activities for visitors to Sarawak is a day's trek along one of its many rivers.

Below This man is an Orang Ulu from Santubong. His home is built in the traditional longhouse style and he is playing an Orang Ulu musical instrument.

Above Unsuspecting insects that stop for a rest in the shade of this pitcher plant (genus *Nepenthes*), are drowned and digested by a liquid produced in its cup.

Right Trekking through some of Bako National Park's terrain can be difficult, especially in mangrove swamps. The park's authorities have built walkways, so visitors can experience Bako's amazing wildlife at first hand.

Above There must be few places in the world where beaches of such unspoiled beauty are so readily available to anyone willing to seek them out. This is Damai beach, just a few metres around the bay from the beach huts and food stalls of the main beach.

Left At Telok Assam in Bako National Park the cliffs have been eroded into outrageous shapes by the weathering of the sea.

Following pages A simple *kampong* by the river en route to Bako National Park. Ferrymen have been handling crafts exactly like these for hundreds of years – why change the system if it works?

West and East Kalimantan

Kalimantan is the largest part of Borneo. Its most easily accessible and culturally distinct area is West Kalimantan, a region quite Chinese in character. Pontianak is a good place to start a trip – once a gold mining boom town, it is characterized along the river by Malay stilt houses and floating produce markets. It is also the setting-off point for a trip along Kalimantan's longest river, the Sungei Kapuas. Two days by riverboat brings you to Putussibau, from where Dayak longhouses can be visited. The longhouses open up the route to Long Apari, in East Kalimantan.

Above Kalimantan is also home to a range of pitcher plants – these carnivorous plants draw their sustenance from insects and can survive in nutrient-poor soils.

Right These Iban villagers are performing a traditional welcoming ceremony. In the background is a longhouse where several families share a common living space.

Left The Dayak tribes of East Kalimantan are facing enormous changes as their region is logged and new towns are built. This boy will grow up into a very different life from the one his father knew.

Above Dayaks living along the Mahakam River, East Kalimantan, depend on the river as a means of transport. Although the people wear Western dress, their houses and the boat drawn up on the bank represent a more traditional way of life.

Left During the course of a riverboat journey, a Bugis mother rests while her baby is snugly supported in an adapted batik sarong suspended from the beam of the riverboat 'taxi'.

Above In 1997 forest fires caused terrible damage to the Kutai Game Reserve, wiping out hundreds of acres of virgin forest and driving out the creatures which lived there. This pig-tailed macaque is one of the lucky survivors.

Above Heteropteran shield bugs *(Catacanthus incarnatus)* are also inhabitants of East Kalimantan's Kutai Game Reserve.

Right A remote reserve on the island, the Gunung Palung Wildlife Reserve in West Kalimantan is made up of 90,000ha (222,390 acres) of virgin forest, mountain springs and thousands of plant and animal species.

Left The longhouses of Tanjung Isuy, a Benuaq Dayak village on the shores of Danau Jempang. In this proud and isolated community, even the steps up to the entrance are beautifully carved .

Following pages Benuaq Dayak women perform a traditional dance at Tamun Jamrot Lamin. The dances incorporate Benuaq customs with those of other tribes in the area, the Kenyah and Kayan.

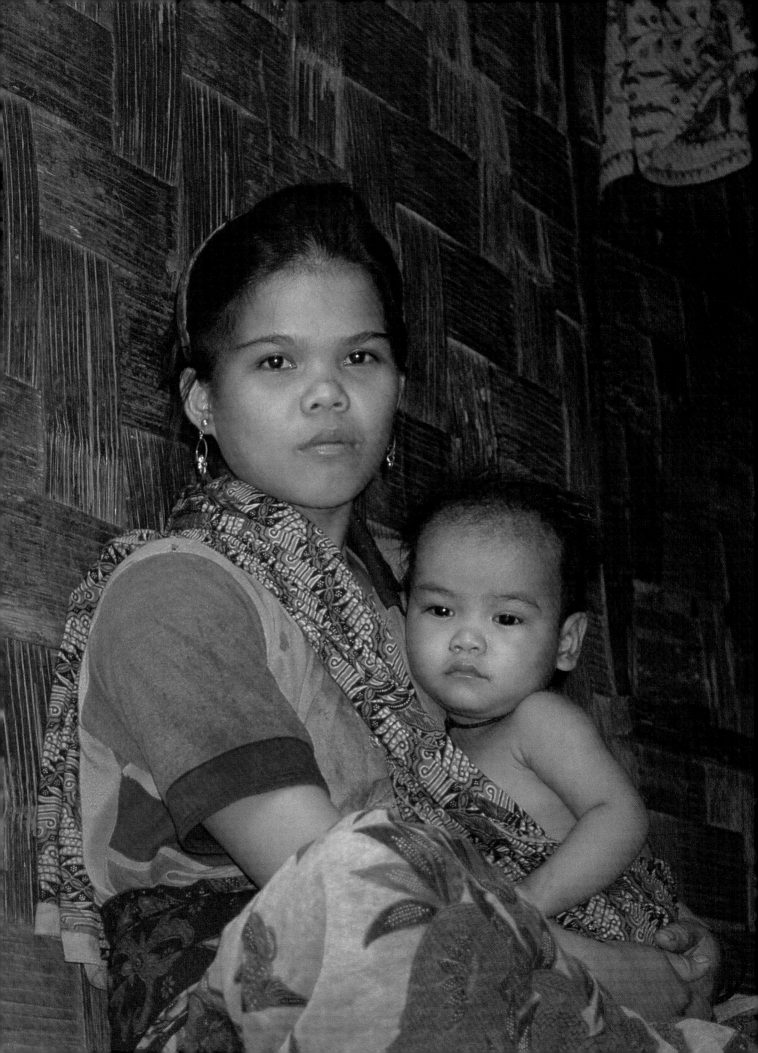

Central and South Kalimantan

Deep in the heart of the island lies Central Kalimantan. The southern part of the region is a vast uninhabited mangrove swamp, while to the north lie the mountain ranges of Schwaner and Muller. Here, travellers will discover a mixture of Islam and animist cultures with very special and unusual festivals such as *tiwah* – the bones of the dead are taken from their graves, washed and ceremonially purified and then transferred to the family mausoleum, a house-shaped stilt box. Central Kalimantan is also home to the Tanjung Puting National Park and the Orang-utan Rehabilitation Centre.

Above The Grand Mosque in Banjarmasin, South Kalimantan. Banjarmasin is a multi-ethnic city and during regional elections in 1997 there were serious racially-motivated riots.

Right A general store in the main thoroughfare of Kalimantan. This old lady will have collected her groceries and provisions in this manner for much of her life.

Left What tourists might collect as souvenirs – batik cloth, *attap* weaving and finely wrought jewellery – are a part of everyday dress in Kalimantan.

Above A species occurring in the peat swamps, the *Vanda hookeriana* is a wild orchid that can be seen near the Sekunir River in Tanjung Puting National Park, Central Kalimantan. It is one of the parent plants of *Vanda miss joaquim* – the national flower of Singapore.

Right A female orang-utan and her baby at Tanjung Puting National Park, a rehabilitation centre for these animals, the only great apes in existence outside of Africa. Without this rescue centre, many orang-utans would not survive the massive deforestation which has taken place in Kalimantan over the last few decades.

Left South Kalimantan is an important area for diamond mining. The workers are dredging a stream bed searching for precious stones or gold particles. A good find can make the prospector a very wealthy person.

Below At Cempaka a 167.5-carat diamond, called *tri saki* (thrice sacred), was found in 1967. There are not only diamonds to be found in Kalimantan's streams and riverbeds; agates are common in addition to gold nuggets and diamonds.

Following pages Sellers and buyers jostle one another as they bargain at a floating market in Banjarmasin, South Kalimantan. The market begins at dawn and is over by 9am.

Above The traditional forms of transport have been turned into a new tourist industry. Intrepid Western travellers are willing to pay a high price for this raft ride along the river.

Above While many Dayaks have converted to Christianity, tribal customs are still carried out, especially in the more remote areas. These are local medicine men and the ceremony they perform is considered to be just as important as any Western medicine.

Left There is much more significance to the rivers than their natural beauty – they also represent the lifeblood of the indigenous people.

Following pages South Kalimantan is predominantly Muslim in character, its population descended from a mixture of Dayak and Malay people. The Malay influence is clearly evident in the newlyweds' elaborate outfits as they sit on the traditional Malay wedding throne.

Copyright rests with the following photographers and/or their agents. Key to Locations: t = top; tl = top left; tr = top right; b = bottom; bl = bottom left; br = bottom right; l = left; r = right; c = centre; cl = centre left; cr = centre right. (No abbreviation is given for pages with a single image, or pages on which all photographs are by same photographer.)

AI Asia Images; **DBL** David Blair; **DBO** David Bowden; **FF** Ffotograff (**LB** Liz Barry); **GC** Gerald Cubitt; **GP** Globe Press (**AE** Alain Evrard; **RM** R Margaillan; **RB** Rieger Bertrand; **HB** H Berbar); **JCP** J Cede Prudente; **JB** John Borthwick; **JS** Jeroen Snijders; **JG** Jill Gocher; **JY** Johansyah Yasin; **MDP** Matt Darby Photography; **MV** Mireille Vautier; **NH** Nigel Hicks; **NPL** Nature Pic Library (**AS** Anup Shah; **DW** Doug Wechster); **OF** Oskar Franklin; **PH** Paul Harris; **RS** Robin Smith; **SCPL** Sylvia Cordaiy Photo Library (**CH** Carda Holmberg; **KH** K Harrison; **SC** Stephen Coyne); **TB** Tibor Bognâr; **TC** Tom Cochrem; **TIPL** Travel Ink Photo Library (**TS** Trevor Smith)

1		JG	18	t	RS	33	tr	GP/AE	54	t	SCPL/CH
2	t	JS	18	b	TIPL/TS	33	b	GP/AE	54	b	TB
2	b	OF	19		JCP	34	t	MV	55		RS
3	tl	JG	20		DBO	34	bl	JCP	56	t	RS
3	bl	JB	21	tl	AI	34	br	JCP	56	b	DBO
3	tr	DBO	21	tr	JCP	35		FF/LB	57	t	DBO
4	t	DBO	21	bl	JCP	36/37		RS	57	b	DBO
4	b	DBO	21	br	AI	38	t	TC	58/59		TC
5	t	DBO	22	tl	PH	38	b	JB	60		JG
5	b	JS	22	tr	DBO	39		AI	61	t	DBL
6	t	GP/RM	22	bl	JCP	40		TC	61	b	NPL/DW
6	b	SCPL/SC	22	br	RS	41	tl	MDP	62		GC
7	t	TC	23		DBO	41	tr	TB	63		GC
7	br	PH	24	t	RS	41	b	MDP	64	tr	GC
7	bl	GP/AE	24	bl	RS	42	t	DBO	64	tl	GC
8		JCP	24	br	TC	42	b	TC	64	b	JG
9	b	OF	25	t	AI	43		TC	65		DBL
10	t	NPL/AS	25	bl	MDP	44	t	NH	66/67		JG
10	b	GC	25	br	GP/RM	44	b	RS	68		JG
11	t	JG	26/27		SCPL/SC	45	t	NH	69	t	JY
11	b	JG	28		SCPL/KH	45	b	JCP	69	b	JG
12	t	TB	29	t	RS	46		TC	70		GC
12	b	JCP	29	b	AI	47		JS	71		GC
13	t	GP/RB	30	t	GP/AE	48/49		AI	72		JG
13	b	TC	30	b	FF/LB	50	t	DBO	73		JG
14	t	JCP	31	t	FF/LB	50	b	GC	74/75		JY
14	b	RS	31	bl	GP/AE	51		DBO	76		JG
15	t	RS	31	br	RS	52		DBO	77	t	JY
15	b	JCP	32		GP/AE	53	t	MDP	77	b	JG
16/17		JCP	33	tl	GP/AE	53	b	TB	78/79		JY

First published in 2003 by
New Holland Publishers Ltd
London • Cape Town
Sydney • Auckland
www.newhollandpublishers.com

86 Edgware Road, London, W2 2EA
United Kingdom

80 McKenzie Street, Cape Town, 8001
South Africa

14 Aquatic Drive, Frenchs Forest, NSW 2086
Australia

218 Lake Road, Northcote, Auckland
New Zealand

ISBN 1 84330 453 8

Publisher Mariëlle Renssen
Publishing managers Claudia Dos Santos, Simon Pooley
Editor Leizel Brown
Designer Lellyn Creamer
Picture researcher Karla Kik
Production Myrna Collins
Cartographer Marisa Galloway
Proofreader Anna Tanneberger

Reproduction by Unifoto (Pty) Ltd
Printed and bound in Malaysia by
Times Offset (M) Sdn. Bhd.

10 9 8 7 6 5 4 3 2 1